Written and Illustrated by Lesley Koplow

Teddy Bear Circle Publications **Copyright 2022**

Wilson and his grandma stopped at the deli for a bagel and hot chocolate on their way to school on a freezing Friday in March. Wilson was happy that he didn't have to wait for the school bus . Every Friday, Wilson's grandma dropped him off at school on her way to her favorite market.

As soon as they opened the door, Wilson saw Ellie the deli cat. She was perched on a shelf above the candy counter.

Ellie was busy surveying her store as customers came in for their morning cup of coffee and bagel. Wilson wished he were tall enough to reach her. Suddenly, Ellie's kitten Popcorn poked her tiny face out from behind Ellie. Then she jumped off the shelf and bounded down to the candy display below to pounce on a little red rubber band that was lying there.

"Next"! called Mr. Murray from behind the counter. Wilson saw that there was one more person waiting before it would be his Nai Nai's turn. He put his backpack down on the floor and watched Popcorn play with her rubber band.

"Wilson"! called Nai Nai. "Come and show me which bagel you want today". Wilson ran to the counter to join Nai Nai. He had 3 favorite kinds, and he wanted to see if they had all of them to choose from.

While Wilson was at the counter, Popcorn was looking at Wilson's backpack. She saw a fuzzy red pom -pom tied to the strap. She wiggled her little body and jumped on the pom-pom . She put it in her mouth with her front paws and pushed it away with her back paws. The pom-pom came off of the string and fell into Wilson's backpack. Popcorn hopped in after it!

When Wilson came back with his bagel in one hand and his hot chocolate in the other hand, Nai Nai helped him put his backpack straps over his shoulders. She noticed that his pouch was open and zipped it shut.

No one noticed that little Popcorn had climbed in!

When Wilson and Nai Nai got to the school yard, Wilson started to feel something poking him through his backpack. At first, he thought it was his superhero toy. Then he reached back and felt Popcorn's sharp little claws poking through the canvas bag! Uh-oh! What if.......
"Popcorn"! Wilson cried out loud, " Nai Nai" ! I have Popcorn!", Wilson called out as he approached the door.

Nai Nai waved goodbye to Wilson. "Eat the popcorn at snack time"! Nai Nai told him, and walked off in the direction of her favorite market.

Wilson didn't know what to do! He didn't think kittens were allowed in kindergarten, but he couldn't walk all the way back to the deli by himself! He decided that Popcorn would have to come to kindergarten for just one day. He would bring her back to Ellie the deli cat when school was over. Ellie might be worried.

Wilson decided to wear his backpack in front of him while he walked up the steps to his classroom. That way, he could protect Popcorn just in case someone bumped into him. He looked around for his friends Jasmine and Tyler and Lilah. He thought he might need their help to take good care of Popcorn at school.

"Good Morning, Wilson," Ms. Aniyah greeted him. Wilson looked startled. He hadn't noticed Ms. Aniyah in the doorway. "Good Morning, Ms. Aniyah," he responded softly. Wilson took off his coat and gloves and put them in his cubby. He decided to hold onto his backpack for a while. He looked around and found Jasmine and Lilah in the book corner.

Jasmine"! Wilson called. " I have to show you something! Come here"! Jasmine skipped over to Wilson. "Look in my backpack"! Wilson whispered. Jasmine peeked inside. "Oooh! A cute little kitten! Where did you get it"? Lilah heard Jasmine's excited voice and jumped up to see what was in Wilson's bag.

"You're not allowed to bring kittens to kindergarten," Lilah scolded. "You're going to get in trouble!" Wilson looked worried. He didn't mean to bring Popcorn to kindergarten. She just decided to come! "I just put my backpack on the floor at the deli for a minute when I went to get a bagel and I didn't notice that Popcorn had climbed inside!" Wilson explained.

"What's going on over there children?" asked Ms. Aniyah. Please put your backpack in your cubby Wilson and go sit on the rug. "Wilson hesitated. Maybe he should tell Ms. Aniyah. " But I have Popcorn"! Wilson replied.

"Well, put that in your cubby too and eat it at lunchtime", said Ms. Aniyah. Lilah and Jasmine started to giggle. Wilson was going to explain, but at that very moment, the principal called over the loud speaker to ask four children at a time to come to the office to pick up their Covid tests.

Wilson had an idea, He took a knit hat out of his backpack and carefully put Popcorn inside. She fit just right all curled up. She started purring and playing with her tail. Wilson took his hat to the rug and put it on his lap. He sat behind Jasmine because she was taller than he was, and would hide his kitten-filled hat. Jasmine sat next to their friend Tyler and whispered the secret about Popcorn, in case they needed him to help. Lilah put one of her hand warmers under the hat to keep Popcorn nice and warm. With popcorn snuggly and happy, Wilson felt all ready for morning meeting.

Suddenly, Wilson remembered that it was his turn to count how many days had gone by since the beginning of the school year! He loved that job! Forgetting about Popcorn for a minute, Wilson stood up to get Ms. Aniyah's attention.

Uh-oh! When Wilson stood up, Popcorn jumped out of the hat. Tyler tried to crawl toward her, but that made Popcorn hiss. Jasmine tried to catch her, but that made popcorn run in the other direction. Daniel G. tried to scare her away from him. He yelled " Woof Woof! I'm a dog"! and jumped in front of Popcorn like a scary dog. Popcorn hissed again, and swatted Daniel's leg. Daniel's leg started to bleed and Daniel started to cry.

Ms. Aniyah scooped up Popcorn. She wrapped her in her scarf and held her in her arms like a baby. She asked Lilah to walk Daniel to the nurse. Lilah took Daniel's hand and led him to the nurse's office.

" Now", said Ms. Aniyah. " Who knows where this little kitten came from"?
 No one answered. Then Sadie said, " I saw the kitten jump out of Wilson's hat"!
Everyone looked at Wilson. He looked at his hat. Finally, he explained about going to the deli and putting his backpack on the floor, and Ellie the deli cat's kitten hopping in when he was at the counter. " Remember this morning when I told you I had Popcorn"? Wilson asked Ms. Aniyah.
" Popcorn is the kitten's name"! Ms. Aniyah smiled and nodded. Now she knew what Wilson was trying to tell her. Wilson felt relieved! . "All right children, we need to go to Library now. Popcorn can play in the supply closet while we are gone". Ms. Aniyah said. Wilson thought Popcorn looked sad.

What happened when Popcorn came to school?

Later, when the children sat on the rug for their goodbye meeting, Ms. Aniyah reminded them about what happened in the morning with Popcorn. " This morning, Popcorn came to school with Wilson. Wilson and his friends took good care of Popcorn. Wilson found a soft place for her to snuggle. Lilah let Popcorn borrow her hand warmer. Everything was fine until popcorn jumped out of Wilson's hat. Who remembers what happened then?"

"Then I crawled Toward her and she hissed"! Tyler said.

"Then I tried to catch her but she was too fast"! Said Jasmine.

"She got scared and hissed", repeated Ms. Aniyah.

"Then what happened after that"? asked Ms. .Aniyah.

"Then Popcorn came too close to me and I freaked out"! said Daniel. "So I tried to scare her away by jumping and yelling"!

" Then Popcorn got so scared that she swatted Daniel's leg and her claws made Daniel bleed"! Jasmine added.

" And then I rook Daniel to the nurse", Lilah said proudly.

" OK class. Today, Popcorn's adventures at school will be your homework".   Ms. Aniyah gave each child a piece of paper and an envelope .

"For homework, draw a picture of a time when you felt afraid, like Popcorn did, but you seemed angry, like Popcorn when she hurt Daniel. Maybe no one even knew that you were really feeling scared! Then, write or dictate a letter to Popcorn about anything you would like to tell her about being with us in kindergarten. Does anyone have a question"?

Many hands went up.
"Are you sure kittens know how to read"? asked Tyler.

"How will Popcorn get our letters? Will we send them in the mail? Will the mailman deliver them to a kitten"? Jasmine asked.

" How did Popcorn get her name"? asked Sadie.

" Can I write a letter to Ellie the deli cat to explain why Popcorn was gone all day"? asked Wilson. Ms. Aniyah wrote the children's questions down to investigate the next day. Then she helped Wilson put Popcorn back in his back pack and walked the children to the school yard. Ms. Aniyah stayed with Wilson to explain about needing to take Popcorn back to the deli on the way home.

Ellie the deli cat was happy to see Popcorn! Popcorn jumped up to be with her mama cat and purred and rubbed against her. Ellie washed Popcorn's fluffy grey fur all over with her coarse red tongue.

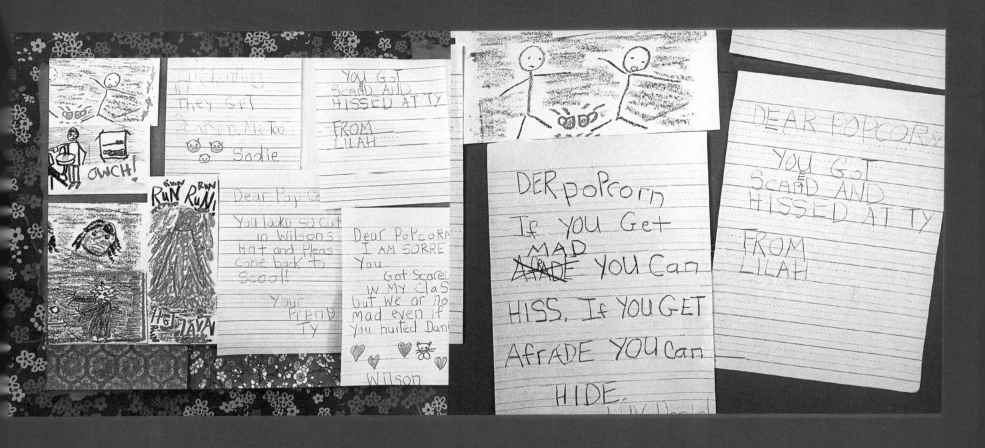

The next morning, the children put their drawings and letters to Popcorn down on the table. Everyone looked at everyone else's letters and drawings, and listened to each child telling the story of their drawing.

"Dear Popcorn, You got scared of Daniel so you scratched him. We still love you".

" I was scared and angry when Covid made my Uncle Matthew died."

" Dear Popcorn, If you get angry, you can hiss. If you get scared, you can hide".

" I was scared when the fire alarm made a loud, loud noise so I hid under the table and wouldn't go outside.. I kicked my pre- K teacher when she tried to pull me out".

" I was scared at the doctor so I was screaming."

" I was scared when Popcorn came too close to me so I shouted and jumped and scared her back".

" Once I was scared at the dentist so I bit his finger."

" It sounds like our class learned a lot from Popcorn! We learned that sometimes feeling afraid is disguised by acting angry, like when Popcorn hurt Daniel after Daniel scared her, and when Tyler got scared at the dentist and bit him. Let's think about that for a while and notice when that happens in our classroom. If someone is feeling afraid, maybe we can help them to feel safer".

" Right now, I have a surprise! We are going to take a walk to the deli so we can deliver our letters to Popcorn! The owner is expecting us to come by. First, everyone take their letters and drawings and put them into this big brown envelope with Popcorn's name on it".

The children clapped. They all put their letters in the big brown envelope and ran to get their hats and coats. They could hardly wait to start walking.

When Ms. Aniyah's kindergarten class got to the deli, they saw Ellie the deli cat up on her shelf, but they didn't see Popcorn anywhere. "Where is Popcorn"? all the children asked.

Mr. Murray the deli man shrugged. "How should I know? She's around here somewhere!
Ms. Aniyah told me you were coming, but I guess I forgot to tell Popcorn"! he chuckled.
The children looked around but nobody saw Popcorn. They all looked very disappointed .

" Let's read a few of our letters to Ellie," suggested Ms. Aniyah. " Then we can leave the rest of the letters here for Popcorn to look at when she comes out".

Jasmine raised her hand. "Can I read my letter to Ellie and then Ellie can read it to Popcorn later"?

"Me too! Me too! " several children chimed in.

Ms. Aniyah chose four children to read their letters to Ellie the deli cat. After reading, each child placed their letter on top of the counter for Popcorn to see later.

Jasmine went first. Ellie listened attentively as Jasmine read.

Then Sadie had a turn. Ellie washed her face with her paws as she listened to Sadie's letter.

Then Tyler had a turn. Ellie rubbed her head on the corner of the shelf while Tyler read, which made Tyler think that Ellie liked his letter best.

Finally, Wilson decided to read his letter to Ellie since Popcorn was still out of sight.

As Wilson started to read, someone opened the deli door and whoosh! A gust of wind blew the children's letters up in the air. Suddenly, out jumped Popcorn from behind the newspaper stand!
She jumped onto the counter to chase the blowing letters. The letters landed on top of her little body. The children all clapped. Popcorn's tiny face and pointy ears peeked out of the paper tunnel. Her tail swished playfully underneath. "Popcorn made a tunnel"! exclaimed Lilah. "Popcorn might not know how to read but she is really smart", said Tyler. " She knows how to play hide and seek"!

Wilson just stood and smiled at Popcorn. Now he knew what made Popcorn feel scared, what made her sad, what made her seem angry, and what made her feel happy and excited.

"Now I know all about Popcorn," Wilson told Ms. Aniyah.   And he did.

Other children's books by this author:

Lilah in the Land of the Littles: A Story for Children in the Time of Covid

Jasmine's Big Idea: Stories for Children in the Time of Covid

Wilson's Wishes: Stories for Children in the Time of Covid

CPSIA information can be obtained
at www.ICGtesting.com
Printed in the USA
LVHW021413190822
726377LV00003B/60